Harrogate College Library
(01423) 878213
This book is due for return on or before the last date shown below.

20 NOV 2008		

D1347873

Leeds Metropolitan University

17 0251821 8

KOGAN
PAGE

29439

YOURS TO HAVE AND TO HOLD
BUT NOT TO COPY

The publication you are reading is protected by copyright law. This means that the publisher could take you and your employer to court and claim heavy legal damages if you make unauthorised photocopies from these pages. Photocopying copyright material without permission is no different from stealing a magazine from a newsagent, only it doesn't seem like theft.

The Copyright Licensing Agency (CLA) is an organisation which issues licences to bring photocopying within the law. It has designed licensing services to cover all kinds of special needs in business, education and government.

If you take photocopies from books, magazines and periodicals at work your employer should be licensed with CLA. Make sure you are protected by a photocopying licence.

The Copyright Licensing Agency Limited, 90 Tottenham Court Road, London, W1P OLP. Tel: 0171 436 5931. Fax: 0171 436 3986.

First published in 1996

Apart from any fair dealing for the purposes of research or private study, or criticism or review, as permitted under the Copyright, Designs and Patents Act, 1988, this publication may only be reproduced, stored or transmitted, in any form or by any means, with the prior permission in writing of the publishers, or in the case of reprographic reproduction in accordance with the terms and licences issued by the CLA. Enquiries concerning reproduction outside those terms should be sent to the publishers at the undermentioned address:

Kogan Page Limited
120 Pentonville Road
London N1 9JN

© Warren Redman, 1996
The right of Warren Redman to be identified as author of this work has been asserted by him in accordance with the Copyright, Designs and Patents Act 1988.

British Library Cataloguing in Publication Data
A CIP record for this book is available from the British Library.

ISBN 0 7494 1920 2

Typeset by BookEns Ltd, Royston, Herts
Printed and bound in Great Britain by
Biddles Ltd, Guildford and King's Lynn

LEEDS METROPOLITAN
UNIVERSITY LIBRARY

1702518218

658.402 RED

Contents

HARROGATE COLLEGE OF ARTS
AND TECHNOLOGY LIBRARY

CLASS   658.402
        RED

ACCESS No. 086330

DATE   LOCATION
27.1.98   HV

CHAPTER 1
What are Facilitation Skills?

Some examples

You're a team leader. It's Monday morning and you are meeting with your team. It hasn't been a bad meeting, as meetings go. You've been through the main items you wanted to discuss and now ask if there is anything else that the members of the team want to raise. Tom says, 'I suppose you realise that we're due to send out the report by the end of this week and I still haven't had the information I need from at least two people here. How am I expected to put all this stuff together without all the material? It's always last minute and I finish up having to work through the weekend.'

It's just what you didn't want to hear. Not that you are surprised, but you hoped this had been dealt with last time. Why don't they learn? And how do you respond?

Well, how *do* you respond? Here are some possible responses:

1. Tell Tom that he'll just have to manage somehow.
2. Ask who hasn't sent in the information and instruct them to get on with it.
3. Say that in future all information for the report has to be in by the due date.
4. Delegate to Tom complete responsibility for ensuring that all the information is in on time.
5. Ask the team to consider how best to deal with the problem and arrive at a decision acceptable both to you

7

and the majority of the team.
6. Suggest to the team members that they should sort this out between themselves.

You may think of other responses. Perhaps you would use a combination of two or more. Decide which is the one that most closely represents how you would handle this situation? Write the number in the box below.

Here is a second example.

You have just asked each member of your team to report briefly on the progress they are making with a project. For the second time, Paula has admitted to having done little. 'I've got too much on my plate. There are other priorities, you know. If I don't keep the customers happy none of us will be in work.'

How do you handle this one? No suggestions from me this time; just jot down your own ideas.

Let's go back to the first example and look at your response to Tom and his dilemma. Any of the responses are ways that might be appropriate for a team leader to use, depending on the circumstances. But only one of them would be consistent with facilitation skills. I'd suggest it's number 5.

What does facilitation mean?

Before you congratulate yourself on getting it 'right' or wonder why you got it 'wrong', give some consideration to two questions.

First, what does facilitation mean? Second, when are facilitation skills appropriate and when are they not?

Write down your thoughts on those two questions now. Use this space if you like.

_____

_____

_____

_____

You'll have realised by now that the process of this book is in itself a facilitating one, as long as you are involved in it.

Facilitation, in this context, means drawing out the ideas, experience and beliefs of a group so that they arrive at conclusions and decisions that are really theirs and that they are willing and able to take responsibility for.

That means that (a) the group members have to be ready to share their thoughts and (b) that they have the knowledge and skills (the competencies) to take any relevant action. It also means that (c) a climate needs to exist within the organisation that encourages team members (and team leaders) to participate in decisions that help them to achieve their own objectives within the context of organisational aims.

Is the climate right for facilitation?

There are, therefore, some important prerequisites before you embark on developing your team through using your facilitation skills. Tick off here whether or not you believe that your team, and the organisation, is ready. Mark each question on a score from 1 to 10. (If you agree completely, score 10; if you disagree, give a low score.)

1. The organisation's management structure is very open. ☐

2. My manager is very approachable and open to ideas. ☐

3. There is an atmosphere of sharing good practice. ☐
4. People are encouraged to learn from each other. ☐
5. I feel supported by my management. ☐
6. My team members are capable of doing their work. ☐
7. Team members are ready to develop themselves. ☐
8. People trust each other within my team. ☐
9. People are good at expressing their views in the team. ☐
10. I feel ready to challenge the team more. ☐

Total ☐

If you have scored 75 or more, your organisation and your team are likely to benefit from and respond well to facilitation skills. In fact, you are probably using some good facilitation skills already and are ready to reinforce your own good practice by polishing up those skills or coaching others to develop theirs.

A score of 50–74 means that you may have some groundwork to do in developing some of the required qualities. Gradually developing and using your facilitation skills will not only improve the effectiveness of your team, it will also have an impact upon other parts of the organisation. You will be in demand!

A score of 25–49 might mean that you have to give yourself a longer time before you can expect results. The effect will, however, be even more significant.

If you scored below 25 the news is not good. You will need to obtain much more support for your ideas before attempting to change the whole culture of the organisation by listening to what your team has to say! Even so, do not despair. By changing your own behaviour with your team, consistently over a continuous period, you will achieve some significant benefits.

The benefits of using facilitation skills

Here are some of the changes that can be highly beneficial to you, to your team, to the organisation and, most important of all, to your customer when your team develops through your facilitation.

- Your team will become more motivated and willing to share their ideas.
- Members of the team will take on greater responsibility for their own and the team's performance.
- The team will learn better ways of dealing with problems.
- Team members will pool resources more effectively.
- Individuals will learn new competencies from each other.
- Newer team members will be brought in more positively.
- Productivity will improve.
- The quality of the team's service will be enhanced.
- New ideas and changes can be accepted and acted on more positively.
- The sharing of ideas for good practice will go beyond the team.
- There can be a positive impact on others within the organisation.
- Your own work-load can be reduced through delegation.
- You will have greater time to attend to managing.

All the above benefits have been achieved through using facilitation skills, as much experience has shown. It is well worth learning how to develop them with your team.

Just before finishing here, I invite you to jot down a real example of your own, of an issue that you have recently faced within your own team. Or maybe one that comes up at your next meeting!

_____

_____

_____

_____

CHAPTER 2
What is a Team?

What makes a group a team?

Before getting any deeper into facilitation skills for team development, we had better make some definitions of what a team actually is. Getting greater clarity here will itself be helpful in understanding how a particular team needs to develop.

A team is, for one thing, a group of people, given for the purpose of this definition that this group could be as small as two. The difficulty may sometimes arise in distinguishing what makes a group into a team.

Some groups

Let's have a look at a few groups (you can add some more if you like in the blank spaces). Decide which ones are, or may be, teams; then identify the characteristics that made you decide.

1. People at a bus stop
2. A football crowd
3. The football players
4. Shoppers in a supermarket
5. The staff in the supermarket
6. Doctors at a medical conference
7. Butterfly fanciers at a conference of their association
8. Members of Parliament

9. Members of a political party
10.
11.
12.

Write down here which ones you think are a team, then what makes them a team.

_____

_____

_____

_____

Characteristics of a team

In my view, a team has five basic characteristics, all of which must be evident for it to be a fully functioning team. These characteristics are:

- the sharing of a common interest;
- to have a common aim and set of values;
- to have common objectives and/or tasks;
- for members to have designated roles and/or tasks;
- the feeling of membership and loyalty to the group.

Some groups may have two or three or even four of these characteristics, yet not be regarded as teams. Some designated work teams may not possess all these characteristics and may therefore not function properly as a team.

Test out these characteristics on the examples given above, including the ones you have added.

1. People at a bus stop are obviously a group but not a team. They have at least one of the characteristics, probably a common interest in catching the bus, but it's unlikely that it goes beyond that.
2. A football crowd could share three of the characteristics: a common interest, possibly common aims and values and probably a feeling of membership and loyalty.

3. The football players may be a classic example of a team. Note that if any of the five characteristics are missing, the team will not be as successful as it might otherwise be.
4. Shoppers in a supermarket are hardly even a group since it's debatable whether or not they share any of the characteristics.
5. The staff in the supermarket on the other hand will be a team if they have all five. Check in your local supermarket next time you're there and see how they seem to measure up.
6. Doctors at a medical conference might well share three of the characteristics, but unless they are there in order to carry out a specific task and designate the roles and responsibilities, they do not constitute a team.
7. Butterfly fanciers at a conference of their association come under the same category as the doctors. The people who organised the conference will, however, be a team.
8. Members of Parliament probably have two of the five characteristics, a common interest and a sense of loyalty. Otherwise, they will be in other teams, depending on their circumstances. Some will be members of their constituency team at election time. Others will be part of a task force team, or of a department.
9. Members of a political party will share common aims and values as well as having a common interest and sense of membership loyalty. But they won't be a team without clear objectives, tasks and designated roles.

Add any thoughts about your own examples here.

10.

11.

12.

Exercise

Take a look at two or three teams in your organisation, including at least one in which you are directly involved. Give them a rating according to the five characteristics and note down your comments about them. This will give you a good idea as to the extent to which they are functioning well as teams and how they might benefit from better facilitation.

Give a score of 0 to 5, where 1 is regarded as very low and 5 as very high. For example, if a team has very clearly defined roles and tasks, you will rate them 5. If a team appears to have little in common in terms of its understanding of aims and values you will mark them 2. If a team has no feeling of group loyalty, give it zero.

Add your comments in the box overleaf or elsewhere. Any team that has an overall rating of 20 or more is likely to be functioning well. Between 12 and 19 inclusive indicates that team development is needed. Below 12 will tell you that this group does not function properly as a team. Plenty of room for improvement!

Facilitation Skills for Team Development

Team title or designation	A common interest	Common aims/values	Common objectives /tasks	Designated roles/tasks	Membership/ loyalty	Comments

CHAPTER 3
Development Through Facilitation

Developing individuals

While this book concentrates on team development, it is worthwhile noting that no team will develop unless its individual members do. Take the example of Tom given in Chapter 1. You'll remember that he was complaining about the lack of information he had received from others in the team and this caused him problems with his own working schedules. From his tone, it was pretty clear that Tom was disgruntled and may have felt that he was being dealt with badly.

It may be an issue for the team to deal with, with your help, but it is also something that Tom needs to handle more effectively and positively.

Developing the team

One of the skills of the facilitator is to be able to focus on an issue that will have implications for the potential development of all the team members. Even though the issue may apparently be of concern to only one person, the alert team leader will recognise the opportunities for learning and improving working practices.

Let's listen in to a conversation taking place in the team. It focuses on Tom's problem, but is used for his and the team's development as well as solving the problem.

Team Leader:	'Tom, could you just say exactly what the problem is here. I'd like the rest of you to listen to Tom so that we can get things clear and make our own suggestions.'
Tom:	'Well, as I said, I just don't have all the information and the report is due in a few days. I don't think people realise that it takes a long time to put all the material in order and make sure that everything is right before printing off the final document. Frankly, I get fed up when this happens every time.'
Team Leader:	'Perhaps you can be more specific, Tom. What exactly do you need from whom and when?'
Tom:	'I need the end-of-month results from Jessica and the latest on the new project from Gary. And I need them now.'
Team Leader:	'OK. Let's have your comments, Jessica and Gary.'
Jessica:	I can't produce the results earlier than this. I don't get the figures myself until later today. The deadline is totally unrealistic. I've told Tom before. We should give ourselves an extra week to get the report out.'
Tom:	'I'm expected to stick to this deadline. It's what the management team wants.'
Team Leader:	Just a minute, Tom, I'll come back to you. But first I want to hear from Gary and then the others.'
Gary:	'We had a meeting of the project team last week, but I haven't seen the minutes yet. I could give you a rough idea if you like, Tom, or I could chase up the minutes and see if I can get them to you for this afternoon.'
Team Leader:	'Before Tom responds I'd like the rest of you to offer your suggestions.'
Stephen:	'It seems to me that the best way is to delay the report. What's going to be the problem if it's a week later? Nobody seems to use it until later anyway.'

Melanie:	'That's not the point. Tom has the job of getting the report out on time and we're letting him down.'
Jessica:	'That's not fair. I can't do anything about it.'
Team Leader:	'There is obviously a lot of frustration about this and a few of you don't feel things are fair. To summarise what I've heard, Tom feels let down, and Gary and Jessica say they can't get the information out until it comes to them. We also have a question as to whether the report is really needed at the end of this week. I suggest that we each write down one thing now that you could do yourself to assist Tom and one thing that the team can act on. Just take a minute.'

The team members write down their ideas.

Team Leader:	'I'll go round asking for your ideas, finishing with Tom.'
Gary:	'Well, I could take my own notes at the meeting and let Tom have them straight away. In fact, I probably have enough to put the main items down now. As far as the team is concerned, I think we could have a more regular update on the report's progress with a clearer timetable.'
Melanie:	'I could assist Tom in some of the compilation of the report. I think I'd quite enjoy that and I'd welcome the chance to have some input. I agree with Gary on the team, it's just what I've put down.'
Stephen:	'I'm not really sure what I can do other than get my information in on time. If it would help, I'd be willing to do some chasing up. I still think we should extend the deadline and that as a team we should request it.'
Jessica:	'I suppose I could try to get an earlier printout of the information, or I could ask my friend in

	sales to give me the figures even before then. It will only bring things forward by a day or two. Maybe Tom could attach a note to the report informing management what the difficulties are. I'm sure we'll all back him up.'
Team Leader:	'Now Tom, you've heard these suggestions. What do you think would be most helpful and what are your own suggestions?'
Tom:	'I think I can help myself by taking up some of those ideas. I'd appreciate Gary giving me his notes rather than waiting for the official minutes. I'll certainly take up Melanie's offer of helping me to put it all together. Maybe we can talk about that for the next one. And if Jessica can get that information in quicker that'll be a lot of help. Even a day makes a difference. I also think it's worthwhile seeing if we can't get an extra day or two. I'd appreciate it if you [looking at the team leader] would do that on our behalf.'
Team Leader:	I'll be happy to do that, Tom, if you will write down the key reasons and the advantages of a brief extension in the future. Is there anything you will do yourself to make things run better in future?'
Tom:	'I'll prepare a clearer timetable and I'll ask for help before it gets too late. And I'll try not to get quite so ratty in future.'
Team Leader:	'Thanks for all of your contributions to this. Let's make a record of what we have committed ourselves to and I shall make sure we review this next time.'

Exercise

Make a note of the facilitation process as you saw it in this example. What were the key things that the team leader did or said and the skills being used?

_____

_____

_____

_____

Now consider a time when you were on the end of a facilitation process. What happened and what was the effect on you and others in the team?

_____

_____

_____

_____

CHAPTER 4
The Skills of Facilitation

Current skills – an exercise

You will have noticed some of the skills used by the team leader in the previous chapter. Go back through the brief excerpt and note them down here.

_____

_____

_____

_____

Now consider the skills you have in relation to facilitating a team. Whether or not you have much experience in this, you will certainly already have a number of skills that can be applied to facilitation. Think about them and note them here. It is not easy to be objective about your own skills, so try not to be over-optimistic nor too harsh on yourself. It would be very helpful to you to get some feedback from someone else who could comment on what you write down here.

Use the grid overleaf to record your facilitation skills and, in the second column, note how and when you have demonstrated those skills. Then share your notes with a colleague or your manager to get some feedback.

	My team facilitation skills	How I have demonstrated these skills
1		
2		
3		
4		
5		
6		
7		
8		

Use another sheet of paper if you need to add other skills.

Facilitation skills: a summary

You will have used your own words for the skills you have. Here are the skills that I suggest are needed in order to be a good team facilitator. Tick off the ones that you have identified, or the ones that are similar in meaning to your own.

1	Listening	The one common skill needed in all good management (and most other forms of relationships).

2	Understanding the team members	Seeing members of the team as individuals, recognising particular traits, strengths and weaknesses.
3	Being clear about objectives	The need for the facilitator to know and understand objectives in working with a team. Relating organisational objectives to the process of facilitating teams to meet those objectives.
4	Setting a contract	Helping the team to arrive at an agreed set of rules for the ways in which it will work.
5	Maintaining control	Ensuring that the process for team development that has been established is kept to.
6	Focusing on development opportunities	Keeping a consistent lookout for any issues that provide an opportunity for the team to develop its ideas and work.
7	Identifying issues	Encouraging team members to determine their own issues for discussion.
8	Participation	Finding ways to encourage full participation by all team members.
9	Clarifying and dealing with problems	Using the members of the team productively in arriving at positive and creative solutions.
10	Summarising skills	Getting the team members to arrive at their own summaries and conclusions so as to ensure that issues are fully understood before reaching decisions.

11	Agreeing action	Moving towards the most appropriate action with the full approval of the team.
12	Encouraging responsibility	Consistently supporting and challenging the team to take on greater levels of responsibility within their roles.
13	Distinguishing between process and content	Being able to concentrate on how the team is working together as well as what they are debating.
14	Keeping an overall picture	Having an understanding of the implications of the team's development in relation to the wider organisation and vice versa.
15	Dealing with problems in the team	Helping the team to face up to internal difficulties and resolve them.
16	Reviewing and evaluating	Conducting team review and evaluation processes in a way that encourages continued development.

Skills required – an exercise

Now that you have considered some of your present skills and looked at a summary of the skills that I believe are needed by a good facilitator, make a note here of the skills that you need to acquire or brush up. Add how you could best do that.

The skills I need to gain	How I can gain them

If you are clear about which skills you have, which you still need and how you can develop them, you will find the rest of this book useful in reinforcing what you are doing. Where you are unclear, the book will give you useful guidelines and exercises to improve your facilitation skills.

The following chapters will take you through in greater depth each of the 16 skill areas. In Chapter 21 we will look at a seven-step process for team facilitation that will assist you in using those skills to develop your team.

CHAPTER 5
Listening Skills

The ability to listen well is probably the single most important skill that anybody needs in order to relate to other people effectively. Most managers still don't recognise this as the case, or, if they do, don't make it apparent!

The facilitator must, above all, be able to listen at several levels. In *Counselling Your Staff*, another book in this series, I outline a structure for listening that can be used in any setting. In this book, I will illustrate the listening process as it relates to team facilitation, describing that in Chapter 21.

At this point, here is a brief summary of the key things to consider when seeing how well you come across as a listener.

Listening is a process

Listening is more than just that. You need to *listen*, to *hear* what is being presented, to *understand* it, to *accept* the person who is presenting something to you and finally, you need to *respond* in some way. Let's go through that again, this time noting the things you can actually do to demonstrate your listening ability.

Listen

To listen properly, you need to be clear that you are listening and intend to listen. For this you have to establish a *contract*. This varies according to people and circumstances. In a team, you will need to establish some rules that say, for example, that people won't interrupt, that they won't be blamed for being open, nor blame anyone else, that they will have time to express their views etc. The contract can also include the items or issues to be discussed; in other words, the agenda.

Hear

In order to hear what people are saying, you need to *identify* the real issues. You can pick these up not only by what people say but also by the way they say them, their eye contact, their body language and by the kind of words and phrases they repeat or reinforce.

As a facilitator, you need to recognise what is going on in the team and to show that you are able to draw out the real issues before they become problematic.

Next time you are in a group (of any sort) see if you are able to identify what is going on and therefore show that you can hear beyond the actual words, as well as the words themselves.

Understand

Going beyond hearing what is being presented means that we have to understand what it actually means, or rather what the other person means. Too often time, energy and eventually money is wasted because of simple misunderstandings. It is easy to make assumptions based on an interpretation of what is said, only to discover later that there were differing perceptions around the room.

How often have you experienced something like this? 'I thought you said the computer was down and you'd asked Maureen to see to it.' 'No, I said Maureen was feeling down and she'd asked me to ask you to get the computer fixed.'

In order to understand properly, we have to *clarify* what is being said. In a team, this becomes even more crucial. It's a case of ensuring that everyone has the opportunity to become clear about what is meant and the implications of that for them.

Accept

The point here is that we don't have to agree with someone to accept the person. What frequently happens is that in disagreeing with someone's view or suggestion, especially in organisations, we appear to put them down, stifling potential creativity for the future.

Once you have clarified what someone is saying, the most productive way to demonstrate acceptance of the person is to *summarise* it. This has the dual effect of ensuring that the person hears it back and also often enables them to take more responsibility for their own action. Within a team, this is a very powerful developmental tool.

Respond

Once someone has been listened to, heard, understood and accepted, something interesting happens. They are ready to take responsibility and ready to take appropriate *action*. Your task, as the facilitator, is to encourage the team to support the action and to be clear about it.

Exercise

Take another look at the listening process described here and in summary form below.

Then practise it, first with one or two people, then in your team. Note what happens, then see what you need to be doing to enhance your skills. It usually needs a bit of practice.

Process	Structure	Practice
Listen	Contract	Agree the 'rules'.
Hear	Identify	What are the real issues to be discussed?
Understand	Clarify	Questions to establish the meaning.
Accept	Summarise	Check that everyone gives feedback of their understanding.
Respond	Action	Ensure that responsibility is taken for appropriate action.

CHAPTER 6

Understanding the Team Members

Team members as individuals

Just like you, each person is unique. If you intend to help your team to develop, you have to be aware of each individual. More important, each person needs to feel that you know, understand and value his or her personal contribution.

You will make it much easier on yourself if you make an effort to know each of the team members. This doesn't mean that you are expected to socialise with them or to know personal details of their lives, unless this is relevant. What it does mean is that you ensure that you give some time and space to having individual interaction.

This can be a normal part of what you do anyway. You may have direct contact with individuals from the start through their interviews and induction. You may be involved with helping individuals to set work plans, or in their appraisals. You might even be involved in disciplinary procedures, or in counselling some members of your team.

The essential thing to bear in mind is that you need to give equal attention to your team members if you want them to regard themselves as being equal members of the team, and to play an equal part in it. Be very aware that you do not want to create, or exacerbate, feelings of ill-will, unfairness or envy within the team.

Recognising traits, strengths and weaknesses

One of the main purposes in seeing your team members individually is that you get to know their traits. If you have an understanding of how individuals behave and see things, then you are more likely to be able to handle their distinct differences positively in the team.

Equally, knowing people's individual strengths and weaknesses allows you to understand the joint strengths of the team and where you may need to encourage additional skills to be developed.

Exercise

Take a look at your team members. As a check on how well you know them, write down their attributes as you see them now. Make up a grid like this for the number of members in your team.

	Team member	Strengths	Weaknesses	Comments
1				
2				
3				
4 etc				

Where you believe you need to know more about some of your team members, put aside time to complete the grid to your satisfaction. Decide how best you want to get the information. Can you create an opportunity from a meeting you are having? Will you make a point of visiting someone while they're working to ask how they're doing? Perhaps you prefer to set up a formal review meeting, or at the other extreme, get together on a very casual basis.

Whatever you do, make the 'getting to know you' experience a positive one. Make it clear, for example, that you want to improve communication and that this means making sure that you listen to individual staff members. You could also encourage people to talk about their view of their work and how the team is doing.

Be open yourself about your intentions and you will receive an increasing level of openness and support from your staff. But do remember that if there has not been much previous communication, and the level of trust is low, it will take much patience on your part.

It will be worth it.

CHAPTER 7
Being Clear About Objectives

Know your objectives

It's a good idea, at this point, to make sure that you know just what you hope to achieve by developing your team through using your facilitation skills. Going back to the section in Chapter 1 on *the benefits of using facilitation skills* can help you become clear about this. Before you begin your work with the team, however, you will need to have some very concrete ideas about your objectives.

For instance, is this a new team of people who need to learn about the work or project they are to undertake? If so, how quickly do you want to get them on stream? Is it a team who seem to be demotivated for one reason or another? If so, what do you want to achieve with them and what is a realistic goal? Perhaps you want to integrate new members, or introduce new methods of working, or improve the rate of production or enhance the service to customers. Whatever the circumstance, you can identify your own objectives very clearly.

But even before becoming clear about your objectives with the team, you must know what the objectives or goals are of the wider department or organisation. In other words, you need to relate the goals of your team to those of the organisation. Obvious; but often missed by team leaders when they go about setting team objectives.

Organisational goals

With luck, you will have these already, or someone will know what they are. If there don't seem to be any clearly specified goals for the organisation (or department) over, say, the next 12 months, your asking the question might raise a few eyebrows and cause someone to think about them.

An example of such goals might be to improve productivity by 5 per cent, or to introduce an additional 400 customers to your company, or open two more branches, or reduce costs by 10 per cent. Anything that is stated as a goal will have an impact on your team, even it it's to maintain the status quo.

Write down some of the key organisation goals here.

Team objectives

Now that you are clear about those goals, and you have a good idea about the individual members of your team, including their strengths and weaknesses, you are in a better position to devise your own objectives for your work with the team.

While the focus of this book is on facilitation skills, it is important that you keep in mind what you want to achieve within the overall goals of the organisation. The danger otherwise is that, while you may become expert at developing your team, they may develop in an inappropriate direction. Too bad if the team gets highly motivated into setting up a new project that doesn't stand a chance of being carried out because it's not part of organisational strategy. They won't thank you for it. Nor will your boss.

Exercise

The next exercise for you to carry out is therefore to write down what your own objectives are over, say, the next 12 months. Since you will probably want to look at this in stages, it may be helpful for you to look ahead, then define more clearly what you realistically hope and expect to achieve in the shorter term.

Objectives for developing team

12 months	6 months	3 months

Use this, or a similar format for yourself and take your suggestions to a colleague, manager or team member so that you can get feedback and refine what you have come up with. You'll realise that, since you are wanting to use a facilitation process, it is healthy to consult openly with your team members on issues like this. The more your team members are involved with defining their objectives, the greater will be their sense of ownership and responsibility in carrying out those objectives.

CHAPTER 8
Setting the Contract

Why a contract?

The essential difference between facilitation and other forms of team meeting is that your task (as the facilitator) is to assist the team in arriving at their own conclusions and subsequent action in respect of issues that are relevant to them. In balancing that with what you want, or the organisation wants, you will need to negotiate your own input.

Negotiation is the word here. You may have things to say, or to request; but you also have to encourage all the members of your team to participate in defining their own rules.

That is where the setting up of a contract is so vital. It sets the scene for the whole facilitation approach and the potential development of your team.

The contract

First of all, let's just imagine what a contract could look like. Here is an example from a real team (taken from *Portfolios for Development*, published by Kogan Page):

- Team members will make every effort to attend these meetings.
- The purpose of the sessions is to enhance individual performance, to improve defined skills, to develop team work and to provide support.
- Individual issues discussed within the team will remain confidential to the group.

- Members will carry out any agreed action and will report on the results of that action to the rest of the team.
- Each member will keep a record of his or her achievements for a portfolio to be shared with other members of the team.
- Members will listen to each other and respect each other's views.
- We will challenge and accept challenges positively.

This contract took some time to set out and was appropriate for this particular team. It was written up by the facilitator on a flip-chart as the agreements were made and put up at each meeting so that members would be aware of what they had decided. It allowed the facilitator to point out whenever team members failed to keep to their own contract and vice versa.

You and your team may have quite a different contract. For example, you may include some of the practical targets that you and the team want to achieve over, say, the next six months. Such things as specific customer improvements, financial goals, project completions and so on can be part of your team's contract. But don't omit the issues to do with how the team conducts its meetings, since that will be a significant factor in the team's overall performance and achievement of practical targets. If you have been clear about the objectives and can help the team to devise their own, as the previous chapter suggested, it will become relatively easy to set up your contract in terms of both content and process (see Chapter 17 for a further discussion of this).

Your contract-setting session

You could establish the team's contract at the first session, or you may introduce the idea gradually. In any case, you should not leave it longer than the third session before at least starting on a contract.

You may have to give the team a few clues about what you are getting at, but don't fall into the trap of offering all the ideas yourself. It will never be theirs then and you would properly be challenged later on with 'Well, they're your rules anyway'.

Preparation

It is a good idea to rehearse how you are going to introduce the notion of setting up a contract with the team, especially if this is going to be a new experience for them (and you).

Be clear why you are suggesting a contract. Know what the purpose is, have an idea of the kinds of thing you can suggest as examples relevant to your team, prepare how you will respond to questions or comments designed (possibly) to sabotage your efforts.

Have a go at writing down your ideas here. If you prefer to use a term other than 'contract', please do so. You might use 'rules', 'agreement', 'guidelines', 'understanding', 'bargain', or simply 'Let's decide how we want to run our meetings'. Complete the following openers:

The purpose of our agreeing to a contract is:

_____

_____

The kinds of thing that we could include are:

_____

_____

The help this contract can be to our team is:

_____

_____

The responsibility for keeping to, or changing, the contract belongs to:

_____

_____

Record the contract

The ideal way to keep a record is to write it up so that everyone can see it as the agreements are made. A flip-chart is excellent for this. Either you can do this or (better still) find another team member to write it up. You can then either get it typed up for everyone or ensure that it's always available at team meetings.

Remember also (and remind the team) that the contract can be added to or renegotiated at any time, and certainly when new members are brought into the team.

The importance of maintaining a record of the contract can't be over-emphasised. It will be the most valuable tool you have to remind the team of how it is performing when you come to review the process. This is dealt with in later chapters.

Exercise in contract-setting

Get together with your team (or perhaps test it out first on a few colleagues who will support and challenge you). Your task is to establish with that group a set of guidelines that will be a contract for:

(a) what your purpose is in meeting together;
(b) how you will run your meetings (a good way of putting this is to ask what people do and don't want from the meetings and each other);
(c) what you want to achieve together and individually.

Now try it out! Remember to ask for feedback from members of the team on how they found the process.

Once you have done it, review your own thoughts and the feedback and jot them down. What did you find that was positive and negative and what have you learnt? What will you do to improve the contract-setting process?

CHAPTER 9
Maintaining Control

What kind of control?

There is a common misconception that facilitating a group means not providing any direction. The reason is that people who are asked to be facilitators may not understand what it means, nor have the skills needed to provide the appropriate direction.

There is a difference between the kind of control an authoritarian manager will want to take and the kind of control maintained by a facilitator.

Have a go here at noting what this difference is likely to be.

_____

_____

_____

_____

Now give some thought to meetings that you have attended, or perhaps run yourself. Give some examples, whether these are within work or anywhere else, and make a note of the kind of control that the person running the meeting kept over the group. Say whether you felt there was too much or too little control or it seemed about right. Then qualify what you have said by noting what made it too much, too little or just right.

Meeting	Control level	Why?

The kind of control that an authoritarian leader may keep is likely to be in the kinds of decision taken. That means that this leader will direct things in the way that he or she wants and tend not to take differing views into account. The focus will be on what is said and by whom rather than on how the members of the group arrive at decisions.

The facilitator/leader will tend to control the way that time is used, ensuring that people participate in discussion more or less equally and that the group keeps on track with its own agenda.

How to keep control

Maintaining control using facilitation skills is easy if you follow the steps set out in this book.

First, ensure that you have fully absorbed and carried out the exercises in the previous four chapters, or at least tested them to your satisfaction. Just to recap, you will have developed your listening skills, got to know more about the members of your team, set your objectives and established a contract with the team.

Second, you will maintain control in a positive sense by carrying out the steps and developing your skills in the ways described in the ensuing chapters.

Third, here are some key things for you to remember:

1. Be clear about what you expect and how you intend to work with the team.

2. Never assume that what you have said has been received. Be assertive (not aggressive) in repeating your messages and in making your requests from the team.
3. Keep the team to its contract. If, for example, the team has agreed not to discuss rumours, remind them clearly if someone begins to do that. If there is an agreement not to interrupt while someone else is talking, make sure that you clearly and firmly point out when there are interruptions. If the team has set a target to carry out a particular task, ensure that you remind them of the agreement.
4. Keep your eye on the issues, or the agenda items being discussed and keep the team on track in terms of the time spent on those issues. But be at least equally concerned about the group process (dealt with in Chapter 17). You are going to maintain control more effectively when, for example, you show your ability in drawing out quieter members and keeping verbose ones from taking up too much time.
5. See yourself as a conductor, with your team as the musicians. Each person has a part to play. You are the only one not playing a tune, but you hold the baton and with it can keep the orchestra playing harmoniously or allow it to disintegrate.

CHAPTER 10
Focusing on Development Opportunities

One of the things a conductor does, in rehearsal anyway, is to stop the orchestra every now and then to review what it has just done and to improve upon it. An authoritarian conductor will tell the orchestra what to do; one who is more of a facilitator will ask the musicians for their ideas.

The results may not be any different in the shorter term. In the long term, the orchestra, or in your case the team, will feel more motivated to develop new ways of achieving consistently better results if you use a facilitation style skilfully.

One of your roles is to make the team aware of its own achievements and to help the members see how they can build on them. Equally, you have a key part to play in getting team members to see how they can transform difficulties into opportunities for development.

An example

Let's take the example of Tom, right at the beginning of this book, and especially the section in Chapter 3. Look back at that conversation in the team. You'll see that towards the end, the team leader asks each person to give their ideas on what they can individually do to assist in dealing with the issue Tom had raised.

Gary said that he'd take his own notes at other meetings

rather than wait until he got them before doing anything about it. Melanie offered to help Tom compile the report. Stephen said he would do some chasing up. Jessica offered to get information earlier. Tom said that he would accept the offers of help and prepare a clear timetable. He also asked the team leader to help by negotiating a time extension. Finally, he said that he wouldn't get 'so ratty' next time.

If you were the team leader, what would you see as the development opportunities arising from this particular issue? How would you take it forward with the team?

_____

_____

_____

_____

_____

Before you read the next section, please have a go at making your response to the foregoing exercise. Then remember that your response is likely to be as valid as mine. The important thing is to experience the process of thinking about the development opportunities that this example can create. If you do that, you will have recognised that this mirrors what you will be asking the members of your team to be doing: think for themselves and empower themselves.

Some ideas

Here are my ideas about potential development opportunities that arise from the team's discussion on Tom's issue. They are in question form, since that may be the way to invite the team to give them adequate consideration.

- How does this show that we could support each other more?
- Is there some way that we can improve our planning process?

- What's the best way to speed up communication from meetings?
- How can we take things forward to management when we have ideas for improvements?
- Where can we develop some partnerships within the team in order to improve specific work projects?
- When team members feel frustrated, how best can this be presented to the team?

Learning from specific examples

The skill of the facilitator here is to help the team move from individual examples of issues raised and problems dealt with. Development means learning from those so that when a similar issue arises, the team is able to handle it without going through the same cycle all over again.

This means that you need to maintain an overview of what is going on and see beyond the specific problems to the bigger potential. Remember the maxim that every problem is a learning opportunity. That way, you will focus on the development opportunities and stop the problems piling up.

CHAPTER 11
Identifying Issues

Who sets the agenda?

One of the ways that managers maintain, or attempt to maintain, control in an authoritarian way is for them to set all the agenda items for meetings. Most managers who do this don't see themselves as authoritarian; it's rather that they have not been aware of alternative possibilities, or may be afraid that things will get out of hand if they don't keep control of the items to be discussed.

This next key skill for the facilitator is to assist team members to determine their own issues for discussion.

Exercise

Consider the difference between the team leader or manager setting the agenda for a team meeting and the members of the team identifying their own issues to go on that agenda.

First, as a manager of a team responsible for running the next team meeting, compile the agenda of items that you believe need to be discussed. Just jot down the main headings.

_____

_____

_____

Now spend a little more time on this second part of the exercise. Go round to members of your team. If you have a large team, select four or five with different ideas and characteristics. Ask them individually to think about what they would like to have discussed at the next meeting. Don't take 'I've no idea, anything you want' as an answer. Challenge them to give some consideration to their own work and how it's going, to any positive or negative things that they see going on, to any ideas they may have had, to things that concern them. You may ask them to tell you what some of those things are or to write them down for you to see at a later date.

When you have compiled a list of the issues that team members have given you for discussion, write them down here.

_____

_____

_____

Now check the two lists.

- Are there differences?
- If so what does this mean?

_____

_____

- If there is no, or very little, difference between the lists, what other differences might there be between the initial process of your writing down an agenda and your compiling one from what the team has said?

_____

_____

The difference

When team members feel that they have been properly consulted and engaged in the procedure for deciding the main items to be discussed, they are more likely to want to be involved in that discussion than if the agenda is presented to them. It is hard to facilitate a discussion when nobody feels any ownership of the issues.

The difference may or may not be in the actual issues put forward. A manager who is familiar with what is going on is likely to be able to raise those issues. The real difference will be in the quality of the discussion, the learning processes that can be encouraged and the desire by team members to become more fully involved in changing things where they need to be changed.

Drawing out the issues in the team

What you have just looked at is one way to engage people in putting forward their ideas for the agenda. Here is a second way.

Instead of preparing an agenda in advance, which may be important in certain circumstances, you may try waiting until the team is together.

The advantage of this is that people are likely to be more spontaneous and creative in their ideas and that you can develop more participation from the start. The disadvantage is that you might see it as risky. What if nobody comes up with anything? What if they come up with things that are too challenging or difficult? What if key items that you believe need attention are left out? What if you are seen as an ineffective leader?

The answers to all these is that you will get it right if you are prepared to take the risk and are clear about your intentions.

Remember your objectives, remind people of the contract; then invite each person to suggest the one or two issues in their work that are the most important to them at this time.

Write up these items on a white-board or flip-chart and then get the team to group them so that you don't have an unwieldy list. You may finish up with eight or nine key items. You can add your own to the list if you want, since you are a member of the team. This is your agenda. More important, it is everyone's agenda.

You don't have to deal with everything at one session. In fact you can invite the team to give them an order of priority. You can tick things off as they are dealt with and add new things as they come up.

Try it. You might have fun and you might discover some new energy in yourself and the team as a whole. But beware: do not use this method simply because you haven't given any thought to the agenda. You still need to prepare to carry out the process and you still need to know what you are doing.

CHAPTER 12
Participation

Clarifying your own role

If you are moving into a facilitating role, this may mean that you intend to be behaving differently in the team. It may also be true that there has been a different style of leadership by the previous manager. Or it could be an entirely new team.

Whichever is the case, if there is any change in style at all, you need to make your own role clear, especially since facilitating means gaining full participation by everyone else.

Write down your role here in relation to how you will be working with the team. Say what you believe in terms of why you are taking on a facilitation role. Say what you will be doing. Say what you hope for and expect of the team. Say what you believe will be the outcomes.

_____

_____

_____

_____

_____

_____

What does participation mean?

One of your roles will be to encourage full participation. Being clear what that means will assist you in reaching that goal. Full participation does not necessarily mean that everyone has to talk in equal portions. Some people are more skilled and comfortable at talking than others. Some take more time up in talking than is healthy for the rest of the group so that others get bored or frustrated at the time being wasted. Some find it hard to talk in a group at all.

Your task is to draw people in when they want to share their ideas and concerns; to prevent others from taking up too much time; to ensure that anyone who has something to contribute has the chance to do so; and to keep the discussion on track in terms of the issue being dealt with.

You will have achieved full participation when everyone feels that they have had that opportunity and when they are satisfied that their ideas and contributions have been properly attended to. This means that somebody could spend the whole time listening rather than talking. The essential thing is that he or she is listening to what is going on rather than spending the time wishing that the meeting would end.

Exercise

Go back to the exercise in Chapter 6 where you were asked to record some of your team members' characteristics. Now think about them in terms of how you see them participating in a group discussion. Who do you think you may need to draw out more? Who might you want to contain? Who is good at listening and asking questions? Who is prepared to challenge? Who seems creative? And so on. Jot your thoughts down in the form overleaf.

Team member	Participation

Practice

Take the next opportunity to practise some of these skills. Here are some ideas:

- When you have your list of issues or agenda, ask each member of the team to say briefly what is of particular interest to them and note this next to the item.
- When you are discussing a specific issue, ask those people to say something about it, inviting everyone to note what is being said ready to respond later.
- Establish a clear time limit with the team for discussion on issues, depending upon their importance and urgency (different things!) and make sure that nobody takes too much of that time. Practise keeping people to the point rather than letting them ramble.
- Watch what is going on in the group. Where you see someone wants to come into the discussion but others jump in first, call on that person to talk and remind the others that they also need to make sure that others aren't left out of the discussion.
- At some time in the discussion, if people seem stuck or ideas are not flowing or people all start talking at once, invite them to stop, jot down their current thoughts about the issue being discussed and then ask everyone to read out

those notes. If people interrupt each other and you don't have a 'no interruption' clause in the team contract, you can suggest that this be added, giving you a mandate to intervene appropriately.

- Have a brain-storming session, where everyone is invited to call out their ideas to solve a particular problem and all these are written up without debate. (More of this in the next chapter.)

Now try out these and any of your own ideas. When you have practised encouraging greater participation with a team, write down here what happened, what you learned and what you still want to improve.

What happened	What I learned	What I want to improve

CHAPTER 13

Clarifying and Dealing With Problems

Where do problems come from?

One of the things that holds organisations of all sizes back is that they spend so much of their time dealing with problems. In other words, they become crisis-managed. There will, of course, always be problems, but where those problems are handled by management passing down directives for change in order to deal with them, or by ignoring them in the hope that they will go away, the problems will become bigger and more significant.

When that happens, the problems are actually caused by inappropriate management practices. The process of facilitation enables problems to be dealt with at the root, at the right time and by the people who are directly involved and affected by them.

Clarifying problems with the team

Facilitation often needs courage. You may find yourself having to face uncomfortable things. They are unlikely to be anything you didn't already know, but perhaps you'd rather not hear it from your team members.

The skill here is not to take anything in a negative light. When someone presents a problem to the team, your first task is to clarify what the problem is and to ensure that everyone understands it.

Practise asking clarifying questions, not interrogatory or defensive ones, and invite other members of the team to do the same. And remember that it's not just what is said, it's the way that you say it that can turn a defensive question into a clarifying one. Try saying 'What exactly do you mean?' in different ways. See what I mean?

Give examples of clarifying questions here.

_____

_____

_____

_____

Example

Helen says, 'Well, since it's my turn I might as well tell you that I'm completely fed up with the delays and excuses in getting my computer upgraded. It's holding up the design work and there's going to be a backlog. I can just see what will happen: everyone is going to blame me for the project falling behind when it's not my fault.'

You could have seen this coming. Helen has been asking you for three weeks and you have been on to the technical department. They have promised, but have pleaded great demands on their time and a lack of staff. Company policy means that everything has to go through the technical department rather than outside firms. Helen is looking at you accusingly.

It would be easy to get defensive on this, or to get angry with the technical department or company policy and side with Helen. Then you could march into somebody's office and demand some action. But your role here is to help your team solve its own problems in as positive a way as possible.

Note down here how you would deal with getting greater clarity from Helen in terms of what the problem actually is.

In this case, Helen, with the help of the team and facilitator, made the following summary.

'I have asked for a computer upgrade from my manager and left it to him to deal with. I haven't actually made it clear what the upgrade entails, or what I really need my computer to do, or the reason for it, or the implications of not having it. I haven't investigated other possibilities either, like seeking other computer operators and checking to see if I could share some time. I guess I just wanted to pass the buck on this one because I was too tied up trying to struggle with my design work on the current system.'

It's worth thinking how Helen came to that greater clarity. Of course, you could say that all this should have been clear from the start, but we know that things often don't work like that.

Arriving at solutions

Once you have facilitated the team to help one of its members become clear what the problem is, you and they are well on the way towards solving it.

One of the ways is to go through a quick brain-storming process. If you are not familiar with that, here is a summary. After that, you can try it out.

Having clarified the problem, write it up on a board or flip-chart. Then ask team members to call out any suggestions they have, however obvious or bizarre they may be, to try to solve the problem. Just write up all the comments, not allowing any discussion at this stage. Everything and anything goes. Make a time limit of two minutes. Even if the ideas stop, carry on until the time is up.

When you have a list, ask the team to pick out three or four ideas that it thinks would work and ask them to discuss the advantages and disadvantages of each. The team will probably come up with a combination of ideas and the action to follow up.

Try it with a problem that your team has presented, perhaps something like the example of Helen and her computer. You could be surprised at the creative ideas and energy that emerge from the team; and the commitment to taking action to improve things.

CHAPTER 14
Summarising Skills

The importance of summarising

One of the most common errors made by managers is the assumption that people have understood what has been communicated to them. This is compounded when apparent agreements are made in the team and only later do you discover that there are different perceptions of what has been decided or even discussed.

Rehearse the scenario. You reached an agreement with the team that the annual stocktaking would take precedence over the sales conference unless there were specific reasons for anyone being in attendance. It was also agreed that, in the event of additional help being needed, staff from the accounting department had offered to assist.

To your surprise, Kevin is absent during stocktaking and you discover he's at the sales conference. At 4.30 pm the team is far from finished. You ask if anyone from accounting has been along and find out that nobody has been asked. Surely it was clear? Wasn't it?

You even thought that you had made a summary at the end of the meeting, but Kevin tells you that he'd assumed that since he had a specific reason, he should go to the sales conference; and the rest of the team said that they'd thought you had asked the accounting staff to come along.

Hearing the summary

Remember the listening process described in Chapter 5? In

order to understand, we need to summarise. The best way of understanding what has been said is to summarise it yourself. That means that for anyone else to understand it fully, they have to summarise it for themselves too.

In facilitating others, instead of just offering your own summaries to the information you have heard, you are drawing information out of the team members and asking them to summarise what they have understood.

Exercise

The task this time is to draw a summary from the members of your team. Next time you are with the team, or handling any meeting, just go round the room at the end of the discussion on a particular item and ask people to make their own summary of what has been discussed.

The most powerful thing to do is to invite each person to write down a brief summary and then to read it out. Everyone might come out with the same thing. The more likely possibility is that you will hear different perceptions. It's important not to treat some perceptions as wrong and others right. The learning point is that there will be different ones and each can add to the others.

If you want an intermediate stage for yourself, I suggest that you make a summary of a particular item at another meeting you attend and ask a couple of colleagues to do the same; then discuss your respective perceptions. Sometimes subtle differences can become quite significant, so that you need to ascertain just exactly what the issues are or the agreement was.

Make some notes here on your experience, either in making your own summaries or in asking your team to come up with theirs.

_____

_____

_____

Arriving at conclusions

Having gained a variety of summaries from the team will enable you and them to see that there may be one, or more than one, understanding of the principal issues. If there is a common perception then you can go ahead quite easily with your next step. If there are several, different and possibly conflicting perceptions, you will need to gain greater clarification.

That is the main point of the summary: to gain greater clarity on anything that is not already clear for everyone. It gives you the chance to check things out by asking people to pay attention to the differences. Then, only when you have made sure that there is a common understanding, you will be able to have the team arrive at the most appropriate decisions.

Note that there is a big difference here between asking people to agree on solutions and asking them to reach an understanding about what the issue or problem actually is. All too often, because of people's own point of view, they will want to jump to a conclusion or decide on the action before hearing what is really at stake.

The process, as you'll remember from Chapter 5 is to get people to listen, to hear, to understand, to accept and then to take action. There are three main effects of asking people to make a summary of what they have heard before commenting on what they think should be done about it:

1. If there is further clarifying to be done, it will be dealt with here.
2. It becomes easier for people to accept each other's opinions.
3. It paves the way for decisions and action.

More practice

Because this is such a crucial skill and one that is under-used, here are two more things for you to do before you leave this section.

First, summarise this chapter and one other chapter that you select. Write down your summaries here.

_____

_____

_____

_____

Next, write down a summary of the last three conversations you had. What were the key themes? What questions do you have from the conversations? Is there anything that you believe needs further clarification? Are there any things you, or the other people, need to be following up or acting on from those conversations?

_____

_____

_____

_____

CHAPTER 15
Agreeing Action

The appropriate response

Facilitation skills are often seen as ones that deal only with the group process. They may even be scorned as not having relevance in the real world (wherever that is), because they don't deal with the things that have to be done. Your goal is to show that facilitation skills are the ones most likely to achieve results.

In a task-oriented environment, action is the only thing that seems to count. As long as we're seen to be doing something, the perception is that there will be some success. The trouble is that action is often taken before knowing whether it is the only, or the best, or the most appropriate response to the original problem or request.

When you go through the process described in this book, you will be more certain that the action agreed will be carried out and that it will be the one most likely to succeed in the shorter and the longer term.

When the team has, with your help, established a contract with one another, identified the issue to be dealt with, clarified what that issue entails and summarised its essence, the action that follows will be an appropriate response to the original issue raised.

Even more significant than that will be the team's ability to work together more productively in dealing with issues in the future.

Individual responsibility

One of the outcomes of facilitating this process will be the greater acceptance of individual team members in taking responsibility for their own actions (or inaction). As facilitator, one of your roles is to ensure that any agreed action is accompanied by an agreement as to exactly who is to take it, and by when.

No longer can things be left to chance, or assumed that someone else (usually you) will follow things up. The person accepting responsibility for a piece of action may need support, and this should be explicitly dealt with as well. Again, it's your task to remind the team that, while an individual may have agreed to carry out something, that person also has the right to call on and expect the support of other team members. If it's not already in the team contract, it can be added at this stage.

Team accountability

From this, it follows that the team itself will become increasingly accountable for the actions (or inaction) of its members and for its successes and failures.

In organisational terms, the team leader is usually the one who is held accountable for the team's performance. The process of facilitation means that accountability is closer to the action rather than higher up the hierarchical ladder. This is development for the organisation as well as the individuals within it.

You may have some questions about this. Write down some of your questions here. Then have a go at answering them, maybe after you have had a conversation with someone else about it. The key question I have for you is: what does it mean for the team to become more accountable within your organisation?

_____

_____

_____

Relevant, realistic and measurable?

Having helped the team to summarise and reach conclusions as described in the previous chapter, you will find it relatively simple to help them to arrive at an agreed action plan. If this isn't so easy, it is probably because the previous stages have not been adequately completed.

Sometimes you will have two or more possible action plans. Even if there is only one, you need to do a final check before letting the team move on.

First, ask the team to check whether the proposed plan actually deals with the issue that it originally identified.

Second, ask them to check how realistic their solution is in terms of the time, the feasibility, the information and the skills needed to carry it out. You may need to point out when, in your experience, people have attempted to take on too much without considering the wider implications.

Third, remind the team to decide how they will measure the success of the action taken. This is as essential for you as it is for the team. Measurements of achievements are going to convince you and the rest of your organisation that facilitation actually works in a very tangible way.

Exercise

The first part of this exercise is theoretical, the second part practical.

First, give your response to this question: what is the difference between the decisions and the action taken in a team meeting that is conducted in an autocratic way as opposed to one that is facilitated? Use your own experience of these two styles in making your comments.

Second, practise with your team the process of helping them towards agreeing action. Remember particularly the issues of individual responsibility and team accountability and also the need to check out the relevance, realism and measurability of the team's decisions. Record your experience of doing this here.

_____

_____

_____

_____

CHAPTER 16
Encouraging Responsibility

Support and challenge

We touched on individual responsibility for taking one's own actions in the previous chapter. This section explores the issue of taking responsibility a step or two further. If you look back at Chapter 4 on the skills of facilitation, you will see that alongside 'Encouraging Responsibility' in the table on p 25, it says 'Consistently supporting and challenging the team to take on greater levels of responsibility within their roles'.

There is a barely disguised additional skill here, that of giving a balance of support and challenge. The facilitator needs to be offering support to team members in assisting them to gain confidence and act on their own abilities. At the same time, the facilitator must be providing a challenge to team members to extend themselves and to move beyond their current levels of competence and responsibility.

This, once again, raises an implication for facilitation skills as an organisational development as well as an individual and a team one. That's why there needs to be an acceptance and a culture within the organisation that encourages facilitation processes. Without that encouragement, concepts like empowerment simply do not become real.

Responsibility and empowerment

While we're on the issue of empowerment, this indicates the difference between taking responsibility for carrying out the tasks expected within one's job and extending this responsibility to include a development of the individual's role within agreed parameters. This fits in with the organisation that sees its mission as achieving excellence in terms of exceeding the expectations of its customers. In this case, the individual team members are being encouraged to exceed the expectation of their internal customers.

Here, your facilitation skills will include the ability to ask challenging questions. These will often come after there has been a resolution of a particular issue, or an action has been agreed or carried out. Your questions will be about extending beyond this issue. Give some examples here of questions you have asked, or could ask, that take things a step further.

_____

_____

_____

_____

Applying this to yourself

There is no better way to test out the effect of your questions than to ask them of yourself. Think about an area of your work, or a more specific task that you have recently undertaken. You may be entirely satisfied with it, or you may believe that you could improve it in some way. Even if you are entirely satisfied, apply your questions to yourself in relation to that task, and answer them as honestly as you can.

Do your questions work? In other words, do they challenge you to consider how to extend yourself? Do they help you to develop different ways of doing or seeing things? Do they make you question some practices? Do they spark off some creative ideas? Do they get you excited about new possibilities?

If your questions do at least some of those things, test them out on another of your tasks, or on another person. If they don't do anything, try out some other questions for yourself.

Exercise

When you are satisfied that you have some good key questions, try them out within your team when you get to that stage. Then record the response and polish up your questions, or the way you ask them.

_____

_____

_____

_____

CHAPTER 17

Distinguishing Between Process and Content

The importance of making the distinction

I have referred to process and content a few times throughout this book. The reason for that is that facilitation skills depend to a large extent on the ability of the facilitator to concentrate on both of those things. Dealing only with process may leave the team floundering and feeling directionless. This may be appropriate in a therapy group, but it won't get the job done! Handling only the content gets the tasks carried out but runs the danger of missing opportunities for development.

Mostly, meetings concentrate almost exclusively on content. The result is that people seldom learn from previous practice, either their own or others', and that work tends to be mostly reactive rather than proactive. Crisis management is often the outcome of ignoring the process and being entirely content-oriented.

Process

It's possible that you have reached this page and are still unclear about what I mean by process. If that's so, you will be relieved to know that my definition follows.

I see process to be *how things happen*. In terms of the team facilitation, this means that you need to be aware of what is going on in the group, or the group dynamics.

Give some examples here of what some of these things might be.

_____

_____

_____

_____

My own list includes the following:

- Relationships between individual team members
- How people listen to or interrupt each other
- Tension within the team
- Energy levels in the team
- The impact of individuals on the team
- The pace of discussion in the team
- The desire or reluctance of team members to deal with certain issues
- Levels of motivation in the team
- Expressions of satisfaction or frustration within the team
- How new members are integrated
- How absent members impact upon the team
- The effect of external pressures on the team members.

These are a few of my own thoughts. You may well have come up with other, different ones, equally valid. Hopefully, my list will encourage you to add more of your own.

Exercise

The best way to learn to concentrate more on the process within a group is to observe what goes on and to record your observations. It's also a way of making your involvement in groups infinitely more interesting.

The next time you are with a group, whether this is in work or any other setting, observe some of the dynamics. Afterwards, jot down some of what you noticed.

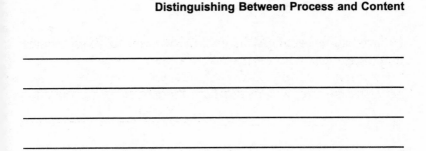

Do this a few times until you become used to it. Your observations will be enhanced if you talk this over with a colleague.

Content

While process is how things happen, content is *what is discussed*. In terms of the team, this will be the agenda and the working through that agenda to arrive at decisions and action.

As facilitator, you need to ensure that the team is clear about the items and issues it needs to deal with and to lead them through those items in a logical and purposeful way. Since it's hard to do that and also keep fully aware of the process, you may choose the option of dividing up the two distinct roles.

This means that, as facilitator, you could concentrate on process and invite someone else to focus on the content. Or you could do it the other way round, asking another team member to keep to the process part.

If you concentrate on content, it is important to be clear about the nature of the issues to be discussed. Are they for information or for action? Are they urgent or important? Don't let the team confuse urgency with importance. If something is urgent but not important the team doesn't need to spend a long time debating it. Help them to recognise the benefits of prioritising items and allocating time limits to them.

Exercise

Invite a colleague, perhaps another member of your team, to

co-facilitate a meeting with you. Decide who will concentrate on content and who on process. Plan how you will carry out your respective roles and how you will assess them. Then have the meeting and record here the main learning points.

_____

_____

_____

_____

CHAPTER 18
Keeping an Overall Picture

Team development and the organisation

Your role as facilitator goes beyond the development of the team. While you need to have a close-up view of what is going on within the team, you also need to have an overview. We can see that as 'helicopter vision'. Imagine yourself hovering above the team, giving yourself a wider and wider view of the terrain.

As you see the team developing, you will begin to see the potential impact this can have on other parts of the organisation.

For example, once the team members take on greater levels of responsibility and increase their communication abilities, people will recognise changes. Other managers will want to know what is going on.

The manager of one team working within a large engineering company decided to adopt a facilitation style of leadership, although this was not the generally adopted management style. His team so improved its performance that the company recognised its benefits and encouraged all its managers to learn facilitation skills. This particular manager had the good sense to set clear objectives with his team and kept a clear record of the changes and achievements to present to senior management. He not only had good facilitation skills with his team, he also had a good overview. He is now a senior executive with the company.

Organisation development and the team

The ability to have helicopter vision works two ways. You will also be able to see that developments taking place within the wider organisation, and indeed beyond this, will have an impact upon the ways in which your team is working.

If, for example, the organisation is going through a process of restructuring, or re-engineering, or introducing any other different management methods, your team will certainly be affected by that. In turn, the organisation will need to be changing as customer demand changes or new products and services emerge.

The team will need to be aware of impending changes, and your role as facilitator is to help team members not only to be aware but to prepare for the implications and take initiatives to deal with them positively.

The learning organisation

What this means is that your team will become part of a learning organisation. Much has been written about the learning organisation, although there are few real examples. Where they exist, they are forward looking and successful, both for the employees and for their profitability.

In essence, the learning organisation is one which facilitates the learning of all its members and continually transforms itself. The facilitation of that learning comes about by teams right throughout an organisation going through the processes described in this book and communicating what they have learned to each other. The facilitation skills of the manager become the most essential of all.

Exercise

To help you to keep an overall picture, here are some questions for you to consider.

- List three main things that your team, or members of the team, have achieved over the past three months.

- What can be learned from this?
- How best can this be communicated elsewhere within your organisation?
- List three things that have not gone as well as you would have hoped.
- What has been learned from this?
- How can you communicate this elsewhere within your organisation?
- List three things that have taken place (or are planned) to change things in the organisation.
- How have you communicated this to the team?
- What has been the response?
- How might you want to improve the communication and response?

CHAPTER 19
Dealing With Problems in the Team

Types of problem

There are very few groups of any kind that will not face some kind of internal problem at some time. Just think of the family group!

When the working group or team has internal difficulties, these can severely hamper the quality of work carried out. Almost all such problems are to do with relationships. The nature of teams is that they consist of different kinds of people, with different characteristics, interests, needs and expectations of themselves and others. It would be too much to hope for that everything will always go smoothly between people. There is almost always bound to be some conflict somewhere.

The manager's job as facilitator is to see the potential and current causes for conflict and help the team members to deal with them constructively.

First of all, it might be helpful to look at some of the types of thing that cause problems within teams. You can probably add some of your own from your experience. Jot down some notes against any of these problems that you recognise within your team.

● **Personality clashes**. Some people just find it hard to accept each other.

- **Envy**. Does anyone seem envious of anyone else in your team?
- **Feuds**. Old arguments and bad feeling re-emerge when they haven't been dealt with properly.
- **Compulsive talkers**. There are those who seem not to be able to stop themselves talking and boring everyone else.
- **Personal relationships**. Sometimes work colleagues also have relationships outside work. This is fine when things are going well, but if they turn sour it can affect the workplace.
- **Misunderstandings**. People often hear what they believe, not what is actually presented.
- **Prejudice**. When manifested, this can cause great discontent. It can be even more difficult when it is subtle and little is actually said.
- **Power seekers**. This is different from showing leadership qualities: this is the attempt to gain power for the sake of it.
- **Different work outputs**. Some members of the team might be slower, or less able than others, causing potential problems.
- **Unfair treatment**. When some members are perceived to have been treated differently or unfairly, team morale can be damaged.
- **Personal hygiene**. Difficult to tell someone he or she smells. They are usually just shunned.
- **Different beliefs**. Only a problem when they come to the fore and cause dissent and discomfort in the team.

The effects of problems

Any one of the above circumstances, or others you can think of, can cause problems that may have a negative effect on the team and its work.

You will note that all of the potential problems outlined above are ones internal to the team, in other words, to do with the group dynamics. There will be plenty of external ones related to aspects of the work, or to organisation problems, such as a lack of resources or technical difficulties. You will be able to deal with those kinds of problem by going through the stages described in earlier chapters, especially Chapters 11, 12 and 13. However, the internal, relationship type of problem may not be defined and may be much harder for people to face and deal with.

As facilitator, your overview and your interest in the group process, as well as the content of any discussion, will cause you to become increasingly aware of underlying problems. More important, you will become more aware of the potential or actual impact of these problems if not dealt with properly.

Exercise

Give some thought to the effect that some of these problems might have on the team and its work.

Dealing with problems

Here are some tips on helping your team to deal with the problems.

Personality clashes	Invite team members to give their observations and feedback to the individuals involved. Get a mutual agreement for resolving things.
Envy	Ensure that each party in the situation is listened to properly.

Feuds	As above. Ask the team to say how this affects them personally and how they suggest it is dealt with. Don't take sides.
Compulsive talkers	Get a time limit set into the contract and keep to it.
Personal relationships	Simply point out any impact you see on the team and its effectiveness and ask the people involved to come to their own agreement how to handle things better.
Misunderstandings	Go through the listening process.
Prejudice	Ask those on the end of any prejudicial behaviour to say what impact this has on them.
Power seekers	Encourage them to say exactly what they want and how they want to get it.
Different work outputs	Ask people to say what support they need and what they can offer.
Unfair treatment	Challenge those who see themselves as victims.
Personal hygiene	Deal with the person individually and directly.
Different beliefs	Demonstrate that any belief is valid, except the one that puts other people down or insists it is the only right one.

CHAPTER 20
Reviewing and Evaluating

Why review?

In a sense, the facilitator is constantly helping the team to review its progress through the process itself. Why then review in addition?

The reason is to ensure that the team is quite clear about what has been learned and the extent to which it has achieved the targets it set out in its original contract. The team can only evaluate its progress against its targets. This will be the measure against which you will be able to communicate the effectiveness of the team's work to the wider organisation. It is a good measure of your own facilitation skills as well.

When to review

You may have different kinds of review at different times. A brief review at the end of each meeting or session you have with the team will serve two purposes. The first is to acclimatise the team to the notion that reviewing what has taken place is, in itself, a worthwhile process. The second is that the review will highlight key points and themes that have emerged during the meeting, will confirm any actions or decisions that have been agreed, will clear up any loose ends and will help team members to recognise the results and implications of their work. This review may last only five or ten minutes.

There may also be a regular, less frequent review that takes a little longer. This will be the one that focuses on specific projects or areas of work carried out by the team. How frequent this is will depend upon your own situation. You might like to jot down here the areas of work that could helpfully have a separate review period.

Work area/project	Review time

Finally, the team would do well to have an annual review. This enables you and the team to look back at the year, to recognise and acknowledge its successes and failures and, most important of all, to see what has been learned and what can be taken forward.

The annual team review and evaluation is something that, in learning organisations, will be used to inform the whole organisation so that this, in turn, becomes part of the company's annual review process.

What to review

If you look back at Chapters 7 and 8, you will see that you have already determined your objectives and helped the team to establish a contract for its working together.

The clearer those objectives are and the more comprehensive the contract, the easier it will be to know what you and the team will be reviewing. It is too late now, and rather pointless, to think about evaluating the team's progress unless you already know the issues and standards against which you are asking the team to make its evaluation.

That is true whether it is the meeting that you have just conducted that is being reviewed, or the work of the team over the past year.

How to review

In facilitating a review, you are using the same methods and skills as with any other facilitating. Recall the meaning of team facilitation identified in Chapter 1. The definition was 'drawing out the ideas, experience and beliefs of a group so that they arrive at conclusions and decisions that are really theirs and that they are willing and able to take responsibility for'.

If you keep that in mind you will know how to conduct a review session. You may, however, find it useful to get your own thoughts together here. Since facilitation is mostly about providing a framework and asking the right questions, that is what is offered here. The framework is the notion of ensuring that a review is always carried out at the appropriate point. The questions are:

1. What will you invite people to review?

_____

_____

2. What questions will you ask?

_____

_____

3. How will you give and invite feedback?

_____

_____

4. What will you record and how?

_____

_____

5. What methods can you think of to encourage full participation?

_____

_____

CHAPTER 21
A Seven-Step Process For Team Facilitation

Introduction and preparation

This process has been developed and used by me and others I have trained for the past dozen or more years with great success. It pulls together all the facilitation skills you need and provides a valuable framework for anyone to use.

In preparation, you need to practise those facilitation skills and in particular, you need to establish a contract with the team that says that you will be working through this seven-step process with them.

This process works best with a team comprising between three and ten people, plus the facilitator. If there are more than this, it is better to divide the team up for the purposes of the process and to have other facilitators familiar with it.

Step 1. Presentation

This first step entails one member of the team presenting a relevant issue of current concern to him or her. It need not be a problem: it may be something that the team member has been thinking about as a possible new project, or it may be a conversation with a customer that raises some questions, or possibly a matter of deciding on priorities, or dealing with new technology.

Whatever it is, it is up to the team member to decide upon its relevance, not you or the rest of the team. This means that anything presented will be acceptable as having significanc and relevance to that person.

I often ask each member of the group to jot down something, ask if everyone has something and then ask wh wants to be the first to present their issue.

When it has been decided who is going first, that perso talks without interruption. You may want to establish a tim limit for this. Five minutes is probably the kind of time you ar looking at.

Step 2. Clarification

Once the presenter has described the issue, invite other member of the team to ask any questions they like in order to clarify wha they have heard. You may need to control this carefully especially when there is a tendency for people to offer thei opinions, give their solutions or describe their own experiences

The essential thing to remember is that, even when thing: appear to be quite clear, there may be as many differen perceptions of what has been said as there are people in th room. What we are seeking here is that the presenter is being properly heard and understood.

The second step is the way towards that, and the more questions asked at this stage, the clearer things will become The person who most often needs to arrive at this clarity wil be the presenter, since usually the reason for presenting something is because there is some confusion.

Your role is to conduct the questions to the presenter and ensure that these are appropriate (in other words designed tc elicit more information and clarity) and to ensure that the presenter has the opportunity to give a response without interruption.

Step 3. Team summaries

When you, the team and the presenter are satisfied that there are no more questions and that the presenter has become clearer about the issue, move on to the next step.

Ask each person (except for the presenter) to write down a brief summary of what the key issues are. Explain that this should capture the essence of what has been said. It is not a verbatim report. Neither is it the time to make any conclusions in terms of the action or decisions that might be taken.

When people have had a chance to write down their summaries, invite each in turn to read this out. The first time you go through this process there may be people who believe that they don't need to write anything down: they can just say it. The outcome is likely to be that those people talk at considerable length and not always to the point. Keep team members to their task of simply reading back what they have written, without embellishment.

Prepare the presenter by asking him or her just to listen to what is said, perhaps noting down some significant points and not to respond to anything at this stage.

It may be that when you ask people to write down their summaries they will suddenly realise that they are not clear and need to ask more questions. They'll soon get the hang of it! Next time they will listen more closely, ask more and get greater clarity.

Step 4. Summary from the presenter

The presenter should now be asked to make his or her own summary. Having heard the others, the presenter is often faced with some different perceptions of the situation. The very process of being heard, then hearing back what you have said, is frequently a liberating one. The person becomes far clearer and finds it easier to accept personal responsibility where that may have seemed difficult before.

When the presenter has made a summary, ask him or her to write it down and then to read it back to the rest of the team.

Step 5. Action from the team

Now ask the rest of the team (not the presenter) to write down what they would do, given the understanding they now have of the issues, the circumstances, the people involved and the personality of the presenter.

Ask people to be concise in their points. Once again, the deeper the understanding of the issue, the easier it will be to come to helpful conclusions about the way forward. You probably need to give people only a couple of minutes for this, then ask each person to read out the action points.

The presenter should be asked to listen and to note anything (presenters often ask team members to hand their own notes to them), but not to respond at this stage. You could also say to the presenter that it is all right to accept or reject anything and that in the end, it is up to the presenter to decide upon the most appropriate course of action.

Step 6. Action from the presenter

Once the other team members have made their suggestions, it is now the turn of the presenter.

It is often remarkable how much the presenter can feel empowered at this stage. What before had been confusing, or had appeared too difficult to face, or insoluble, now becomes manageable. There may even be completely new ideas that have been formulated. The point is that the person directly responsible for an area of work has been supported by the rest of the team, through the process, to accept full responsibility and take action that will develop that work.

Once the presenter has declared what action he or she will take, it is important to ask what further support may be needed to ensure that the action is carried forward.

Step 7. Process review and wider implications

This may seem to be a time-consuming process, since you are dealing with one person's issue and everyone is concentrating on that. My experience, every time, is that the process itself allows other team members to realise how they can deal with some of their own work more effectively. Not only that, but issues that at first appear to be simply the concern of one person may frequently have far-reaching implications for the rest of the organisation.

As this stage the real learning and the potential for considerable development occurs.

- With the team go through the seven steps that you have just guided them through and ask for their feedback about the process.
- Ask the team to consider any implications for their own work and how they might change anything.
- Invite recommendations from the team, based on what they have just learned, for others within the organisation to consider.
- Finally, ensure that both the presenter and the rest of the team agree what the follow-up to the action will be; in other words, when the action and outcomes will be reviewed.

CHAPTER 22
An Exercise in the Seven-Step Method

Example

First, here is a real example of the seven-step process in action. This was a team of area managers in a nationwide hairdressing organisation. The extracts are taken from my book, *Portfolios for Development*, also published by Kogan Page.

1. Presentation
Tim presented the following:

> 'Having established a good training programme and having linked it to our award system for best trainee hairdresser of the year, I've found that three of my eight branch managers are just not supporting it. They say that they'd rather train their people themselves and not have them keep going off for a day every week, especially when they have a lot of trainees. The problem is they put up a good economic argument, but I'm not happy that standards are as good as they should be. The other thing is that the staff in those salons see themselves as above everyone else, so they don't even regard our awards as being an incentive.'

2. Clarification
Some of the questions asked by the team were:

- 'What is your relationship with those three managers?'

- 'What do you think it is about those three branches that makes them feel superior?'
- 'What have you actually said to them?'
- 'What do you mean when you say the standards are not as good in their training?'

Those questions and others were answered by the presenter until each of the team was satisfied that they understood what the main factors were.

3. Team summaries
Here are some samples of what team members wrote down and then read back:

- 'Tim said that he is having difficulty in persuading three of his branch managers to fall into line with his training programme. He feels intimidated by them and doesn't want to upset them. He is not certain in any case that they are wrong.'
- 'The problem that Tim has presented lies in his uncertainty with the training and award scheme. He has not been able to make a positive case to put to his managers and is letting their action undermine his confidence in the scheme. He has not asked them for their views on the programme.'
- 'Tim has got five of his eight managers involved in the training programme. The three others have not taken part and Tim is concerned that their standard of training does not conform in a number of small respects to what is required. Tim sees that the managers have a case, but as yet has not been able to persuade them or himself that his programme is better.'

4. Presenter's summary
Tim's summary was:

'I realise that I feel intimidated by these three managers, who have all been in the job longer than me. That has stopped me from putting forward strongly the benefits of this training programme for their branches and the whole company. I am clear about it, but I have not got that across. The other thing it has prevented me from doing is asking them how they could support the programme. My main concern is that we have a cohesive programme supported by all so that all trainees get a good experience of our training and take a pride in working for the company, not just their own branch. I haven't put that across at all.'

5. Action from the team
Some of the action ideas read out were:

- 'Write a memo outlining the main advantages of the training and award scheme and ask all the managers to respond to it.'
- 'I'd meet the three managers individually and put to them why I want the programme to succeed and ask them what their objections really are. If there are strong objections, I would work out a compromise, asking for half of their trainees to come on the scheme for a trial period.'
- 'I think Tim has to develop a much better understanding with these three managers. I would ask for their assistance and ideas as to how to make this work; or for their suggestions as to how to improve it.'
- 'I would run the scheme as it is for a year. If it's good I'd try to get it company policy that everyone takes part; then they would have to be involved.'

6. Presenter's action
This is what Tim said:

'I'm going to meet with each of the three. I'll write down what I want to say first. I will say what the point of the programme is and its benefits. I will also say what my concerns are, about a common training experience of high standards and about their non-involvement and "separatism". I'll also say that I need their support for the scheme to be fully successful and that I understand their own staffing problems. Then I will ask for their ideas on how to reach our goals.'

7. Process review and wider implications
In terms of the process, some of the comments were:

- 'I really felt listened to and it was amazing how I realised what I had or hadn't been doing.'
- 'It was much easier than I thought being able to summarise what Tim said, because that's all I had to concentrate on.'
- 'It wasn't like any other kind of meeting. There didn't seem to be any competition and it was very supportive, yet we didn't pull our punches.'
- 'We kept to the task well. The structure really helped with that. It seemed very forced at first but it would never have worked without it.'

In terms of implications, some of the comments were:

- 'Tim should carry out his action and report back on progress to the team.'
- 'We need to get on better terms with some of our branch managers. Our communication is very patchy and I think we spend too much time with the ones we get on with rather than the ones we have difficulty with.'
- 'We don't use the experience of some of our really good managers because we probably do feel intimidated by them. In future I'm going to ask for more of their ideas and support and I think we should agree that we all do that and how we're going to do it.'

Follow-up

The outcome was reported by Tim later:

'I carried out my plan. It just worked out that I met first with the manager I find the most difficult. I kept to my brief and I kept my head. By the end of our meeting I felt he had mellowed considerably, although he was still very cautious about getting involved and he was adamant about his training being better, or at least as good as anything else we offered. When I invited him to do some of the training he resisted, but I'm sure he felt pleased. We left it that we'd discuss it more next time. I didn't mind that because I wanted to see the other two first anyway. In fact, both of the others seemed easy in comparison. They had a lot of criticism about the training programme, but both agreed to get involved as long as we worked out a more convenient rota system and they had replacements where needed. They both said they would actually like to do some of the central training and I have fixed them into the programme. I'm certain that the first manager will now want to come in on the same basis. I think the difference was that I listened to them and was clearer with them about what I wanted to achieve.'

The others in the team reported on similar areas of communication that they had had with their own managers, some noting real improvements, others just reinforcing what was already good practice.

Practice

Now is the time to put all your facilitation skills to use. Try out the seven-step method with your team, or with another group first if you wish.

First, make sure that you are familiar with the steps. Write them down, or, better still, write them up on a flip-chart or white-board so that you can refer to them, in conjunction with your team, when you are going through the process with them.

When you have tried it out once, write down your own review and what you have learned here.

_____

_____

_____

_____

Then try it again and make your review, noting what you will want to improve upon. It will be even more beneficial if you talk it through with someone else also skilled in facilitation methods. In this way you are using facilitation skills for yourself.

CHAPTER 23
Conclusions

Summarising the key skills

After all this, I should really ask you to summarise the key skills for yourself. But, if you have done all the exercises already, you have probably done enough!

So I will just remind you of the skills outlined in Chapter 4 and dealt with in more detail in the subsequent chapters. What you can do is to fill in the second column with your own understanding and comments, referring back to the earlier table if you want to.

Listening	
Understanding the team members	
Being clear about objectives	
Setting a contract	

Facilitation Skills for Team Development

Maintaining control	
Focusing on development opportunities	
Identifying issues	
Participation	
Clarifying and dealing with problems	
Summarising skills	
Agreeing action	
Encouraging responsibility	
Distinguishing between process and content	

Keeping an overall picture	
Dealing with problems in the team	
Reviewing and evaluating	

Team development

The whole purpose of this book is to assist you in your facilitation skills so that the team can develop.

You will have become clearer about the areas in which the team needs to develop and you will have seen those developments take place as you go through the facilitation process. Remember that the process is beneficial only so far as there is some actual movement. This is where the content and the process coincide. While facilitation is a process, the results will be in the content. Always keep that in mind and you will maintain your awareness of the tangible results that you want to achieve.

Empowerment

Tangible results will be measurable against the objectives of the organisation, such as increased sales or productivity, improved service provision, reduction in customer complaints, higher profitability and so on.

The ways in which those tangible results are achieved are just as important to the continuing health of the organisation and its members. Increasingly, companies are recognising the value of their people, seeing them as their greatest asset. In order to make best use of that asset, the best needs to be brought out in those people.

This means empowering people to decide upon their own objectives, within the overall framework of goals, to enable them to reach their own decisions and to work in the way that is most beneficial and productive for them, again within the overall framework.

Developing the team through the process of facilitation will almost certainly lead to the empowerment of the team and its members. Within a culture where this is accepted, the opportunity for continuing positive change is going to be welcomed and valued. Where the culture is not so open, the change could be even more significant in the longer term, although harder to achieve.

Developing your skills

Facilitation skills are in great demand. As you use them more and more you will be recognised as someone special; a leader who can draw out the best in people. This won't happen overnight.

Sometimes things will go well, so well that you feel exhilarated by the experience and totally confident that you can do this work. Sometimes things will go badly and you'll wonder what you are doing. I have found that there is one constant thing about facilitating: there is always more to learn.

Always leave yourself some time to reflect on what you have just done, on how you could improve something and on the support you need to assist you in that improvement. Once you develop all the skills outlined in this book, you will be able to adapt them, with additions, to a whole range of uses, including mentoring, coaching, counselling and just becoming more receptive to what others are presenting.

Finally, remember that the development of those skills happens through practice and learning from that practice, not just by reading this book.